AF573933

CELEBRATING HOLIDAYS
Valentine's Day
by Rachel Grack
BLASTOFF! 2 READERS
BELLWETHER MEDIA • MINNEAPOLIS, MN

Note to Librarians, Teachers, and Parents:

Blastoff! Readers are carefully developed by literacy experts and combine standards-based content with developmentally appropriate text.

Level 1 provides the most support through repetition of high-frequency words, light text, predictable sentence patterns, and strong visual support.

Level 2 offers early readers a bit more challenge through varied simple sentences, increased text load, and less repetition of high-frequency words.

Level 3 advances early-fluent readers toward fluency through increased text and concept load, less reliance on visuals, longer sentences, and more literary language.

Level 4 builds reading stamina by providing more text per page, increased use of punctuation, greater variation in sentence patterns, and increasingly challenging vocabulary.

Level 5 encourages children to move from "learning to read" to "reading to learn" by providing even more text, varied writing styles, and less familiar topics.

Whichever book is right for your reader, Blastoff! Readers are the perfect books to build confidence and encourage a love of reading that will last a lifetime!

This edition first published in 2018 by Bellwether Media, Inc.

Library of Congress Cataloging-in-Publication Data

Names: Koestler-Grack, Rachel A., 1973- author.
Title: Valentine's Day / by Rachel Grack.
Description: 2018 edition. | Minneapolis, Minnesota : Bellwether Media, Inc., 2018. | Series: Blastoff! Readers: Celebrating Holidays | Includes bibliographical references and index. | Audience: Ages: 5-8. | Audience: Grades: K to Grade 3.
Identifiers: LCCN 2017029520 | ISBN 9781626177550 (hardcover : alk. paper) | ISBN 9781681034607 (ebook)
Subjects: LCSH: Valentine's Day–Juvenile literature.
Classification: LCC GT4925 .K64 2018 | DDC 394.2618–dc23
LC record available at https://lccn.loc.gov/2017029520

Editor: Paige V. Polinsky Designer: Tamara JM Peterson

Printed in the United States of America, North Mankato, MN.

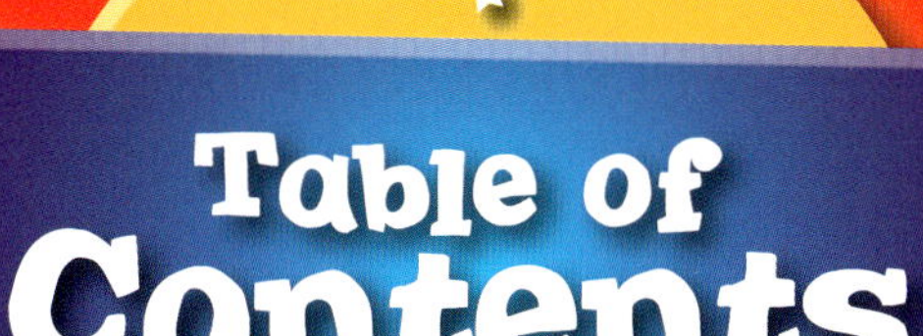

Valentine's Day Is Here!

Children **exchange** tiny cards. Inside, they find candy hearts that say "Be Mine."

They giggle at the silly love notes.
It is Valentine's Day!

What Is Valentine's Day?

Valentine's Day honors the **priest** Saint Valentine. He became a **martyr** for love.

People show their love for others on this day.

Who Celebrates Valentine's Day?

People enjoy Valentine's Day all over the world.

Valentine's Day in Malaysia

Couples celebrate **romance**. Friends and family members exchange gifts, too.

Valentine's Day Beginnings

Long ago, Roman **emperor** Claudius II banned marriage.

Valentine marrying a couple

A priest named Valentine wanted to help people in love. So, he married couples in secret. The emperor sentenced him to death.

In prison, Valentine wrote a letter to the girl he loved. He signed it, "from your Valentine."

How Do You Say I Love You?

Saying	Pronunciation
Italian Ti voglio bene	tee VO-lee-o BEN-ay
French Je t'aime	zhuh TEHM
Spanish Te quiero	tay KYEHR-o
German Ich liebe dich	eesh LEE-beh deesh

Valentine died on February 14 around the year 270.

Time to Celebrate

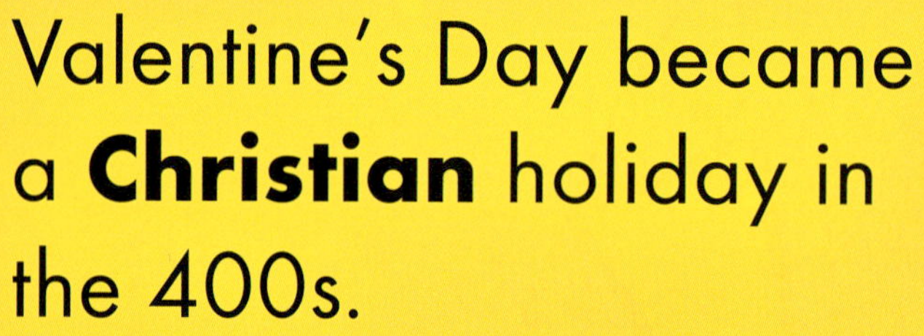

Valentine's Day became a **Christian** holiday in the 400s.

Valentine's Day celebration in London, England

Today it is celebrated by
many different people.
It falls on February 14.

Valentine's Day Traditions!

People trade cards or love letters.

Many are decorated with hearts. Some picture **Cupid** holding a bow and arrow.

Some couples get **engaged** on this day. Many go out for special dinners. They often give each other gifts.

Make Lovebird Valentines

Send sweet notes to your friends with these beautiful birds!

What You Need:

- white paper plates
- scissors
- newspapers
- red, pink, blue, and white craft paint
- paintbrushes
- red, white, and orange construction paper
- pencil
- red marker
- glue
- googly eyes

What You Do:

1. Cut a paper plate in half. Each half makes one lovebird.
2. Set the plate halves upside down on the newspapers.
3. Paint the plates in Valentine's Day colors. Let dry.
4. Draw two small hearts on the red paper. Cut them out. These will be the tail feathers.
5. Draw two teardrop shapes on the white paper. Cut them out. These will be the wings.
6. Draw bird legs and beaks on the orange paper. Cut them out.
7. Write a sweet note on each wing using the red marker.
8. Glue wings, beaks, tails, legs, and googly eyes onto the plates as shown.
9. Give the valentines to your favorite lovebirds!

Some people give red roses to their sweethearts. Others give boxes of chocolates.

Valentine's Day is a sweet reminder to show love!

Glossary

Christian—related to Christianity; Christians are people who believe in the teachings of Jesus Christ and the Christian Bible.

Cupid—the Roman god of love; Cupid was believed to shoot arrows at people's hearts, making them fall in love.

emperor—a ruler

engaged—promised to be married

exchange—to trade

martyr—someone who dies for his or her beliefs

priest—a person who leads religious services and ceremonies

romance—the feeling of being in love

To Learn More

AT THE LIBRARY

Lee, Sally. *A Short History of Valentine's Day.* North Mankato, Minn.: Capstone Press, 2016.

Owen, Ruth. *Valentine's Day Sweets and Treats.* New York, N.Y.: Windmill Books, 2013.

Trueit, Trudi Strain. *Valentine's Day.* New York, N.Y.: Children's Press, 2014.

ON THE WEB

Learning more about Valentine's Day is as easy as 1, 2, 3.

1. Go to www.factsurfer.com.
2. Enter "Valentine's Day" into the search box.
3. Click the "Surf" button and you will see a list of related web sites.

With factsurfer.com, finding more information is just a click away.

Index

The images in this book are reproduced through the courtesy of: Oredia Eurl/ SuperStock, front cover; jenifoto, p. 4; ZUMA Press Inc/ Alamy, p. 5; Zvonimir Atletic, p. 6; Kamil Macniak, p. 7; Aizuddin Saad, p. 8; kirin_photo, p. 9; Fine Art Images Heritage Images/ Newscom, p. 11; Zvonimir Atleti / Alamy, p. 12; Elena Schweitzer, p. 13; Terrie L. Zeller, p. 14; Anna Latimer/ Alamy, p. 15; schegi, p. 16; Niday Picture Library/ Alamy, p. 17; Syda Productions, p. 18; Tamara JM Peterson/ Bellwether Media, p. 19 (all); elenaleonova, p. 20; JumlongCh, p. 21; Nataliya Turpitko, p. 22.